LUFTWAFFE AT WAR

Defeat in the West 1943–1945

As an emergency measure in 1943, Messerschmitt Bf 110G night fighters were pressed into service in daylight against American heavy bomber formations. The extra weight of radar and black boxes and an extra crewman, as well as the drag of the radar aerials, seen here on this Bf 110G-4, reduced performance considerably. Untrained for day fighting, many valuable night fighter crews were lost.

LUFTWAFFE AT WAR

Defeat in the West 1943–1945

Mike Spick

Greenhill Books
LONDON

Stackpole Books
PENNSYLVANIA

Greenhill Books

Defeat in the West, 1943–1945
first published 1998 by Greenhill Books,
Lionel Leventhal Limited, Park House,
1 Russell Gardens, London NW11 9NN
and
Stackpole Books, 5067 Ritter Road, Mechanicsburg,
PA 17055, USA

© Lionel Leventhal Limited, 1998
The moral right of the author has been asserted

British Library Cataloguing in Publication Data

Spick, Mike
Defeat in the West, 1943-1945. - (Luftwaffe at war; 6)
1. Germany. Luftwaffe 2. Airplanes, Military -
Germany 3. World War, 1939-1945 - Aerial
operations, German 4. World War, 1939-1945 -
Campaigns - Western Front
I. Title
940.5'44'943

ISBN 1-85367-318-8

Library of Congress Cataloging-in-Publication Data

Spick, Mike.
Defeat in the West, 1943-1945 / by Mike Spick.
    p.   cm. — (Luftwaffe at war ; 6)
ISBN 1-85367-318-8
1. World War, 1939-1945—Aerial operations, German.
2. Germany. Luftwaffe—History—World War, 1939-
1945. I. Title. II. Series: Luftwaffe at war ; v. 6.
D787.S66   1998   97-38294
940.54'4943—dc   21CIP

All illustrations are via Bruce Robertson except where
otherwise stated.

Designed by DAG Publications Ltd
Designed by David Gibbons
Layout by Anthony Evans
Edited by Tony Hall
Printed in Singapore

LUFTWAFFE AT WAR
DEFEAT IN THE WEST, 1943–1945

As the first day of 1943 dawned, the Third Reich stood at a crossroads. In the East, the German forces had finally been halted, then driven back, leaving 90,000 men of the 6th Army encircled outside Stalingrad with no hope of relief. In the Western Desert the Axis forces were in disarray following their defeat at El Alamein, while behind them massive Anglo-American landings in Algeria and Morocco ensured that the expulsion of the *Deutsche Afrika Korps* and its Italian allies from North Africa was only a matter of time.

Only at sea, where the U-boats of the *Kriegsmarine* were cutting a deadly swathe through Allied merchant shipping, did the situation look more hopeful. In Western Europe, with little or no surface contact between the opposing forces, the Luftwaffe held the ring in what was an almost exclusively a defensive action. By night, RAF bombers pounded targets in Germany itself, although the effects of this had yet to become critical. By day, two *Jagdgeschwader*, JG 2 *Richthofen* and JG 26 *Schlageter*, based in a wide arc between Belgium and Brittany, guarded the Occupied Territories against the increasingly fierce assaults by the RAF, and to a lesser degree, the USAAF. Further to the north, protecting German naval bases, was a third fighter unit: JG 1.

Defensive operations had been no part of the original plan for the *Luftwaffe.* It had been created to fight fast-moving offensive wars of short duration. Consequently its reserves had been small. As at 1 January 1943, insufficient resources had been allocated for the introduction of new and significantly better aircraft and systems, while the training programme remained inadequate to meet the demand for pilots, both in numbers and in quality. Above all, the German High Command was still, at this late stage, refusing to accept the possibility of having to fight a major defensive campaign.

These factors bedevilled the *Luftwaffe* fighter defence of Occupied Europe and the homeland during the final years of the war. Of the many adverse effects, the decision to give bomber production a high priority was particularly pernicious, as it ignored a cardinal principle of war, which is security of base. In fact, *Luftwaffe* bombers played a peripheral role in the war from this point on, and concentrating on their production became a major wastage of effort and scarce resources. This would still have been the case even if an effective strategic bomber had entered production. As it was, the only real attempt at producing such a machine, the four-engined Heinkel He 177 *Greif*, was a failure.

Another waste of resources was the priority given to transport aircraft. The need had been shown by the successful air supply operation at Demyansk in 1942, and was underlined by the lack of sufficient airlift capability to maintain the encircled 6th Army outside Stalingrad. Concentration on bomber and transport production ensured that fighters came a poor third. Only later, when the deadly threat to the Fatherland became impossible to ignore, did production of defensive aircraft improve.

The introduction of radically new types involved new production jigs, tools and lines. Inevitably production of existing types suffered while the changeover was made. As a general rule, quantity took precedence over quality, which meant that modifications to existing models were preferable to the introduction of a new type, with its attendant 'debugging', and often prolonged service entry. Yet improved performance and hard hitting power were still required. This resulted in expedients rather than proper solutions.

As at January 1943, German fighters in the West consisted of two main types: the Messerschmitt Bf 109G (although a few Bf 109Fs remained in service), and the Focke-Wulf FW 190A.

The Bf 109, the prototype of which had first flown in September 1935, was by this time distinctly middle-aged. It had been progressively re-engined to give greater power and performance, and up-gunned to give greater hitting power. Had it been a trifle larger, its airframe could have accommodated these modifications rather better. Never easy to fly at any time, the increased engine torque and weight made it very tricky to handle during take-off and landing, and many inexperienced pilots were lost because of it. At the same time the increased wing loading significantly reduced its turning capability.

The FW 190A, the prototype of which first flew in June 1939, was in many ways better. Whereas the Bf 109 was a rather delicate thoroughbred, the FW 190A was a rough and tough cavalry horse. Wing loading was relatively high, but roll rate was outstanding, as were dive and climb characteristics. It had two major failings: above 7300 m, performance started to fall away; while a high-speed stall came without warning, and was so violent that control was easily lost. This inhibited many pilots from using the full capability of their fighter in a low-level dogfight.

In a purely defensive role, either type could match the RAF Spitfires of the period if properly handled, and they were armed heavily enough to knock down any medium bombers they encountered. Their task was not, however, purely defensive. Each of the Channel *Geschwader* (JG 2 and JG 26) had a *Jabo* (fighter-bomber) *Staffel* attached, which escorted by standard fighters, made hit-and-run raids across the Channel at wavetop height. This was a far cry from the massed bomber raids of 1940, but it was at least a token offensive.

On 20 January 1943, the two *Jabostaffeln,* escorted by over sixty fighters from both *Geschwader*, actually reached as far as London before being intercepted in force by over 200 Spitfires and Typhoons. Losses were high; eight pilots were posted as missing and nine aircraft were written off, for only four claims against RAF fighters. This daring raid, which caused only nominal damage, including a bomb which struck a school at Lewisham, was of more nuisance value than anything else. It was repeated on 11 March 1943, with even less success. Several full-strength raids were flown against coastal targets during spring 1943 but with equally poor results. In late March the two *Jabostaffeln* were reassigned to SKG 10 (*Schnellkampfgeschwader*/fast bomber unit) to carry on the assault.

Luftwaffe attacks were not confined to fighter-bombers in daylight. *Luftflotte* 3 was the command area for France and the Low Countries. For night attacks, *Kampfgeschwader* 2 had about sixty Dornier Do 217Ks and Ms, whilst KG 6 had a similar number of Junkers Ju 88A-14s available. On 17 January 1943, 118 night bomber sorties were flown against London: the first major raid since May 1941. Six aircraft were lost.

A raid on London in similar strength was mounted on 3 March, but once again little damage was caused. Night attacks on other targets followed, but heavy losses, twenty-six aircraft of KG 2 alone during the month, made these an uneconomic proposition. On 14 April, ninety-one bombers raided Cheltenham, then on 16 April, II/SKG 10 tried a high-level night attack on London with twenty-eight FW 190As. It was a fiasco. Little damage was caused, and three aircraft landed at West Malling in Kent in error, thinking they had already crossed the Channel. A fourth crashed nearby, and two more failed to return. Further raids by II/SKG 10 followed, but the bomb load and drop tanks reduced performance of the FW 190A to the point where it could be caught by Mosquito night fighters. On 16 May, two 190s were shot down and another two damaged by Mosquitos of No. 85 Squadron. Then in mid-June, two *Gruppen* of SKG 10 were sent to the Mediterranean, leaving just one on the Channel coast. Attacks by this unit were hereafter reduced to mere pinpricks, although sporadic attacks by twin-engined bombers, led by I/KG 66 using Pathfinder techniques, continued.

The two *Jagdgeschwader* JG 2 and JG 26 had defended the Channel coast of France since 1941, with a great deal of success. Then in the final months of 1942, a new and formidable adversary appeared. This was the Boeing B-17 Flying Fortress, in service with the US 8th Air Force. Bristling with 0.50 in heavy machine guns, and flying in close formation for mutual protection, the Fort posed problems never previously encountered. Its sheer size made judging range difficult, and many *Jagdflieger* broke off their attacks too early for fear of collision. Against massed formations, the traditional fighter attack from astern was hazardous, involving running the gauntlet of a storm of return fire from the heavy machine guns of the bombers.

Egon Meyer, *Kommandeur* of III/JG 2, was the first to evolve a viable tactical system against the US heavy bombers. His method was to fly parallel to establish the enemy speed and course, then accelerate ahead before turning in to attack from head-on.

The early USAAF raids were against targets in Occupied France, but it was not long before the Third Reich itself came under attack. On 27 January 1943, sixty-four B-17s and twenty-seven B-24s raided the German naval base at Wilhelmshaven. They were intercepted by the FW 190s of JG 1, but difficulties in estimating range made these ineffective. Only three bombers went down, against seven German fighters. But as the German fighters took the measure of their new opponents, and even deeper penetrations were made, bomber losses rose.

Initially Allied fighter escort was provided by RAF Spitfires and USAAF Thunderbolts, but these were limited in range. All the German fighters had to do was to wait until the escorts turned back before attacking. But even then, the difficulty lay in the lack of hitting power. On average, twenty hits with 20 mm cannon were needed to bring down a B-17. Attacking from head-on, with barely two seconds firing time, this was far beyond the capabilities of the average *Luftwaffe* fighter pilot. Something far more destructive was needed to get consistent results.

Aerial bombing was tried, but the difficulties of accurate aiming resulted only in a few lucky hits. Then 21 cm mortars, carried in 'stovepipe' launching tubes beneath the wings, were also tried, but once again, the difficulty of judging range accurately, combined with a gravity drop of about 61 m, equally militated against accurate aiming. In any case, these weapons significantly degraded performance and manoeuvrability to the point where a fighter carrying them was a 'dead duck' if caught by the escorts. The real answer was the 30 mm Mauser MK 108 cannon, the destructive power of which was such that only three or four hits were needed.

Initially, the *Luftwaffe* relied on peripheral defence, with a handful of *Gruppen* scattered around the border of the Third Reich. It was, however, soon realised that centralised defence in depth was the only answer, in part because this allowed the defenders to wait for the escort fighters to turn back.

The most heavily-armed German fighter of the early war period had been the twin-engined Bf 110 *Zerstörer*. Unable to live in the same sky as single-engined fighters, by 1943 it had largely been relegated to night operations. Against unescorted bomber formations it gained a new lease of life. While this was fine for the few daylight Bf 110s still available, they were not enough. In a desperate expedient, dedicated night fighters were also flung into the battle. The result was inevitable. Radar-equipped night fighters and their highly trained crews were lost, at a time when the RAF night bomber offensive was really getting into its stride. As American might grew, new units were formed, notably JG 11, while reinforcements from other theatres were drawn in to defend the Fatherland.

Had the status quo continued, it is just possible that the *Jagdflieger* might have contained the American daylight offensive. On 17 August, a massive force consisting of 377 B-17s, in two waves, set course for Schweinfurt/Regensburg. Against it, the *Jagdflieger* mounted over 500 sorties, with many fighters flying twice. American losses were sixty, with many more badly damaged. A repeat raid by 291 B-17s on 14 October met even rougher handling, with sixty bombers shot down, seventeen written off on return, and 121 suffering varying degrees of damage. The *Jagdflieger* had shown that they could inflict unacceptable losses, and the second Schweinfurt attack was the last unescorted deep penetration raid of the war.

This was not to continue. Gradually the range of American escort fighters was extended into Germany itself, culminating in January 1944 with the superb P-51B Mustang. A combination of a low-drag American airframe coupled with a British Rolls-Royce Merlin engine, this not only had the range to go all the way to Berlin, but had the performance and manoeuvrability to meet the German fighters on equal terms. From this moment the defenders could no longer get a free run at the bombers; now they had to fight every inch of the way. Casualties were horrendous; more than 1000 German fighter pilots were lost in the first four months of 1944.

The *Jagdflieger* were on the horns of a dilemma. They needed heavy armament to knock down the bombers, but the extra weight and drag of this reduced performance and made their fighters unmanoeuvrable. But to counter the escorts, light and agile fighters were needed. The solution adopted was a compromise: the *Gefechtsverband*. This consisted of a *Sturmgruppe,* with two *Begleit-gruppen*. The *Sturmgruppe* flew the FW 190A-8/R8, armed with two 30 mm cannon, two 20 mm cannon, and two 12.7 mm heavy machine guns, and was heavily armoured in the engine and cockpit areas. Its function was to attack the bombers from astern, braving the defensive fire. The *Begleitgruppen* flew the Bf 109G-10, a standard fighter, the function of which was to keep the USAAF escorts away from the heavy fighters.

The theory was good; the practice less so. By this time the *Jagdflieger* were heavily outnumbered, and the Bf 109 *Gruppen* ended up fighting for their lives and unable to protect the *Sturmgruppe* properly. By the middle of 1944, they had lost control of the skies over Germany, never to regain it.

The *Luftwaffe* had not entirely abandoned the offensive in the West. Operation *Steinbock* commenced on the night of 21/22 January 1944, when 227 bombers set out to raid London. These included the new Junkers Ju 188s and Heinkel He 177s. Little damage was caused and forty-three bombers were lost, sixteen of them to night fighters. More raids followed against London and other targets, with poor results. The last manned air raid on London took place on 18 April, during which North Middlesex Hospital was hit.

The final *Luftwaffe* assaults on Britain were later carried out by the Fieseler Fi 103 flying bomb, generally known as the Doodlebug. These began on 13 June, with the weapons launched from ground sites, but as these were overrun after the Allied invasion, they were supplemented from the first week of July by air-launches from Heinkel He 111s of III/KG 3, based in Holland. In all, over 9000 Fi 103s were launched, though with so little accuracy that they had little effect on the course of the war.

Meanwhile, it had long been evident that the Allies were preparing to invade Europe. *Feldmarschall* Erwin Rommel, the famed commander of the *Deutsche Afrika Korps*, was in charge of organising the ground defences, while the *Luftwaffe* made contingency plans to reinforce the area when the invasion started.

During the two months prior to the invasion, the Allies flew no less than 98,400 counter-air sorties. Against this the *Jagdwaffe* managed a mere 34,500, during which time they lost 1246 pilots. The *Jagdflieger* were bleeding to death. Not only did they fail to spot the massive invasion fleet across the Channel, they did not even detect its sailing. On D-Day, the Luftwaffe managed to mount a mere 100 sorties, against an Allied air umbrella of more than 3000 aircraft operating in relays.

Worse was to follow. Over the next three months, the *Jagdwaffe* mounted an average of 354 sorties per day, losing an average of thirty-nine fighters per day in the process: nearly seven fighters for each Allied aircraft destroyed. The reinforcement plans fell to pieces; designated landing grounds were bombed, forcing most units to land where they could, while the communications network broke down entirely. German pilot quality had fallen; about forty FW 190As of II/JG 6 tangled with an equal number of P-38 Lightnings, losing sixteen of their number for seven of the enemy.

Chaos reigned. In the confusion of the retreat from France, units based themselves where they could, only to be driven back almost at once. Communications and ground control were virtually non-existent, while from August 1944, fuel shortages added to the problems. Only the stalling of the Allied offensive in the autumn due to logistics problems enabled the *Luftwaffe* to stabilise and regroup.

By 12 November 1944, over 3000 fighters had been mustered. All was ready for a return to the offensive. It was not to be. Many units were frittered away in the Ardennes attack in December, and even more in the abortive New Year's Day offensive of 1945. The *Luftwaffe* never recovered.

Even though the *Luftwaffe*'s organisation was failing, the latter half of 1944 saw several new German fighters enter service. Of the conventional types, the FW 190D, known to the Allies as the 'long-nose', was by far the best. A high-altitude variant, the Ta 152, was introduced before the end of the war, but saw little action. The ultimate variant of the Messerschmitt Bf 109 was the K model. Fast and agile, this featured a clear-view canopy, and was, apart from the 109F, the best of the breed.

Less conventional was the Dornier Do 335. The problem in achieving fighter performance was always how to get the power of two engines for the drag of one. The Do 335 *Pfeil* solved this problem with a tandem layout: a conventional engine in front, and a second, driving a pusher propeller, astern. Had it entered service, it would probably have been the fastest conventionally aspirated fighter of the war. Evaluated in the spring of 1945, it was too late to enter service.

Too late and too few must also be the verdict on the *Luftwaffe*'s jet and rocket-powered aircraft. The twin-jet Messerschmitt Me 262, armed with four 30 mm cannon, which entered service in September 1944, was potentially a world-beater. Very fast, and with a sparkling performance, its main weakness was its engines, which were underdeveloped and very short-lived. In action it was ground down by vastly superior numbers of inferior Allied fighters. Much the same can be said of the Arado Ar 234 jet bomber, which entered service at about the same time.

A notable attempt to combine quantity with performance was made with the Heinkel He 162 *Salamander,* an austere single-engined fighter designed for mass production, and intended to be flown by semi-trained pilots. Although supplied to service units from January 1945, it saw little action.

Point defence was an area which exercised the *Luftwaffe*. The Messerschmitt Me 163 *Komet* rocket fighter had an outstanding rate of climb – 3.35 minutes to 12,097 m – but an endurance measured in minutes only. Unstable fuels led to many accidents, and it accounted for more of its own pilots than those of the enemy. Another interesting but even more suicidal concept for point defence interception was the Bachem Ba 349 *Natter*. Rocket-propelled, this used vertical take-off to save interception time. It never entered service.

Outnumbered and overmatched, the *Luftwaffe*, despite having developed many radically new and technically advanced aircraft, a victim of its own leadership, went down to defeat in the West.

Below: A Focke-Wulf FW 190G fighter-bomber seen with two Junkers Ju 188s, which clearly show the revised tail and long-span pointed wings of this type, although neither has a bulged bomb bay, almost certainly indicating that they were used for reconnaissance. Interestingly, all the aircraft have the spiral spinner markings used for identification in daylight. (*Jeffrey Ethell collection*)

Top left: A rather battered Messerschmitt Bf 109G sits disconsolately outside an Allied building labelled 'Enemy War Material'. After a career of reducing Allied aircraft to scrap, it now awaits a similar, if more inglorious, fate. (*Jeffrey Ethell collection*)

Below left: The Mistel 3 combo, consisting of a Focke-Wulf FW 190A fighter perched atop a Junkers Ju 88G. Faster Mistel combinations were proposed, among them the Arado Ar 234C carrying a Fieseler Fi 103 Doodlebug, and the Heinkel He 162 carrying the Arado E.377, a purpose-built twin-jet pilotless machine. (*Jeffrey Ethell collection*)

Above: During the final months of the war, concealment was the greatest aid to survival of the *Luftwaffe*. Here a Messerschmitt Me 410 peeps coyly out from its cover, as an American jeep drives past. Camouflage, however, was no defence against the airfield being over-run. (*Jeffrey Ethell collection*)

Above: Engineless and tail-less, a Heinkel He 111H, once the symbol of *Luftwaffe* bombing might, lies helpless on its airfield. Its final missions were transport, and air-launching Fi 103 Doodlebugs. (*Jeffrey Ethell collection*)

Opposite page: The best *Luftwaffe* fighter to enter service in any numbers was the Focke-Wulf FW 190D-9. This example is from the Second *Gruppe* of an unidentified unit. (*Jeffrey Ethell collection*)

Top left: The most versatile *Luftwaffe* aircraft of the war was the Junkers Ju 88 series. Seen here is the Ju 188, which started life as a bomber, later became a night fighter, and carried out reconnaissance missions almost to the end of the war. (*Jeffrey Ethell collection*)

Left: The Messerschmitt Me 262 was the first jet fighter in the world to enter service, but its overwhelming performance also caused tactical problems. Featured is a machine of III/JG 7, one of the handful of units with which it served. (*Jeffrey Ethell collection*)

Above: A heavily camouflaged Mistel 2 awaits the call to action. In this case it never came. Vulnerability in daylight and aiming difficulties at night meant that the Mistel concept achieved little. (*Jeffrey Ethell collection*)

Above: Minus its canopy and spinner, this Focke-Wulf FW 190A-8, almost certainly of II/JG 26, stands forlorn on a former *Luftwaffe* airfield. Behind it is a Messerschmitt Bf 109G of the Second *Gruppe* of an unidentified unit. (*Jeffrey Ethell collection*)

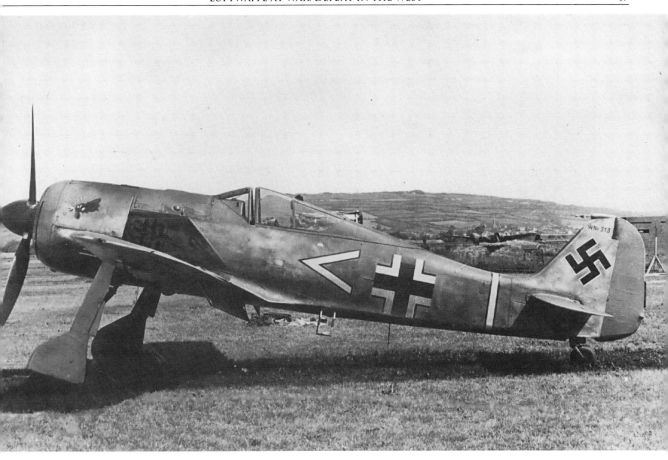

Above: When the Focke-Wulf FW 190A entered service in 1942, its performance and rate of roll caused problems for the RAF, to the point where the British planned to steal one. The RAF's problems were solved on 23 June 1943, when Armin Faber of III/JG 2 became disoriented in combat, mistook the Bristol Channel for the English Channel, and landed his FW 190A-3 in South Wales, giving his opponents an aircraft to evaluate. (*Mike Spick*)

Below: A Focke-Wulf FW 190A of II/JG 26. This was one of the fighter units which from 1941 to 1944 held the ring on the Channel coast against Allied air attacks. To their opponents, fighters of this *Gruppe* for some considerable time were known as 'the Abbeville Boys'.

Above: Introduced to service in 1941, the Messerschmitt Bf 109F (*Franz*) was the nicest-handling of the 109 series. However, the quest for increased performance meant that by 1943, most of them had been replaced by the Bf 109G (*Gustav*). Featured is the Bf 109F-5, a drop tank increasing its effective range.

Below: By the beginning of 1943, the Messerschmitt Bf 109G series had almost entirely supplanted earlier models. With wheels and flaps down, it had to be flown at full throttle even when landing. These are two Bf 109G-4s of an unidentified Reich home defence unit.

Above: Two Messerschmitt Bf 109G-2s await delivery at the production centre at Regensburg in 1943. The USAAF made determined attempts to reduce German fighter production, one of the most concerted being the two-pronged attack on Schweinfurt/Regensburg in August that year. It had little effect.

Below: An example of German ingenuity. The size of bomb carriage on single-seater fighters was always restricted by the aircraft's ground clearance. The Messerschmitt Bf 109G-2 fighter-bomber overcame this with an jettisonable undercarriage leg set amidships. It did nothing for ease of ground handling.

Opposite page, top: In 1941 a replacement for the Bf 109 was planned; the aircraft was to be 25% faster and 85% longer-ranged than its predecessor. This was the Bf 309, which featured a pressurised cockpit and a tricycle undercarriage. First flown in mid-1942, various technical problems were encountered, while handling was less than ideal. In mid-1943 further development was abandoned.

Above: In mid-1943, development of the Bf 309 was abandoned in favour of the Bf 209, the prototype of which was the Bf 209V-5, seen here with the so-called 'Galland hood', and powered by the DB 601A engine with an annular radiator. Although promising, it was dropped in 1944 in favour of the more potent FW 190D-9.

Left: As early as 1937, shortcomings of the Messerschmitt Bf 110 resulted in a replacement design, the Bf 210, which first flew in September 1939. Longitudinal instability was poor, and a single fin and rudder assembly was fitted. Results were still far from satisfactory, and development was halted in 1943 in favour of the Me 410. This is the Bf 210V-13 prototype.

Above: The Arado Ar 232 was the forerunner of the modern military transport. The pod and boom configuration allowed rear loading through clamshell doors aft, while a multi-wheel undercarriage allowed it to 'squat' for loading. The first two prototypes, one of which is seen here under the designation of Ar 232A-0, were powered by two BMW 801A radial engines.

Below: A shortage of BMW 801As led to the adoption of four Bramo radials coupled with an increased wingspan, resulting in the Ar 232B, of which only twenty were built. Known by the *Luftwaffe* as *Millipedes*, they served until the end of the war.

Above: A direct descendant of the pre-war Dornier Do 17, the Do 217E-2, differing from the E-1 mainly in having heavier armament, entered service early in 1942, and took part in the infamous Baedeker Raids of that year, against towns of historic interest in England. A few remained operational into 1943.

Below: The Dornier Do 217M-1 entered service in 1942 at the same time as the Do 217K, and was active in raids on Britain during 1943–44. It differed only from the Do 217K in having two liquid-cooled DB 603 engines in lieu of BMW 801D radials. The machine seen here served with KG 2.

Left: The Heinkel He 111 first flew in February 1935, and at the end of the war four *Gruppen* were still operational, although these were transports rather than operational bombers. Seen here is a He 111H-6 torpedo carrier; the type which cut such a deadly swathe through convoy PQ 17. The final sub-type of this variant was the H-23 transport, which entered production in 1944.

Left: The Heinkel He 115 floatplane was developed well before World War II, and remained in service almost to the end. Its primary task was dropping mines in sea lanes at night, and so effective was it that it was put back in production late in 1943, at a time when the priority for fighters was becoming obvious. In all about 500 were built.

Lower left: From 1943 the Focke-Wulf FW 200 *Kondor* concentrated on anti-shipping attacks, with two *Staffeln* based at Cognac and Bordeaux, and one at Trondheim in Norway. Structurally weak, it suffered heavy losses in landing accidents. Only 252 were built between 1940 and 1944, and in the final eighteen months of the war most were used as transports, for which they had originally been designed.

Above: When it became obvious that the Messerschmitt Bf 210 was a failure, the next step was the Me 310, with a pressurised cockpit and more powerful engines. This was subsequently abandoned in favour of the Me 410 *Hornisse*. The *Hornisse* was essentially the Bf 210 with DB 603A engines. Featured here is the Me 410A-1 fast bomber, with rearward-facing guns in remotely-controlled barbettes.

Below: This Messerschmitt Me 410A-2/U1 was a bomber destroyer, armed with two 20 mm MG151/20 cannon and two 30 mm MK 103 cannon in the bomb bay. Whilst effective against unescorted American heavy bombers, it was very vulnerable to single-engined fighters.

Above: The Me 410A-3 was the reconnaissance variant of this splendid aircraft. Overall, Me 410s operated against Britain from May 1943 and against the American heavies from about the same time. Production ceased in September 1944, by which time 1160 examples had been delivered.

Below left: Rearward-facing armament on the Bf 110G was demonstrably inadequate for defensive purposes, consisting only of twin machine guns. **Below right:** Two 30 mm MK 108 cannon in the nose of the Bf 110G-4/R-3 were quite adequate to deal with B-17s and B-24s, provided that they could be brought to bear. In the presence of single seat escort fighters, this was a dubious proposition.

Above right: The Junkers Ju 88B-0 differed from the standard bomber variant in its reshaped and extensively glazed nose. Whilst the Ju 88B series did not enter production, the reshaped glazed nose was adopted for the Ju 188. This particular aircraft briefly operated against England with the *Aufklärungsgruppe* of the *Oberbefehlshaber der Luftwaffe*.

Below: Not all *Jagdflieger* were patriotic. On 9 May 1943, Herbert Schmidt and Paul Rosenberger deserted, landing this fully equipped Ju 88R-1 of 10/NJG 3 at Dyce in Scotland. They had flown intruder sorties over England in 1940–41, then defensive sorties over Germany, with a marked lack of success. Whether their defection was an attempt to avoid an infantry posting to the Russian front has never been revealed.

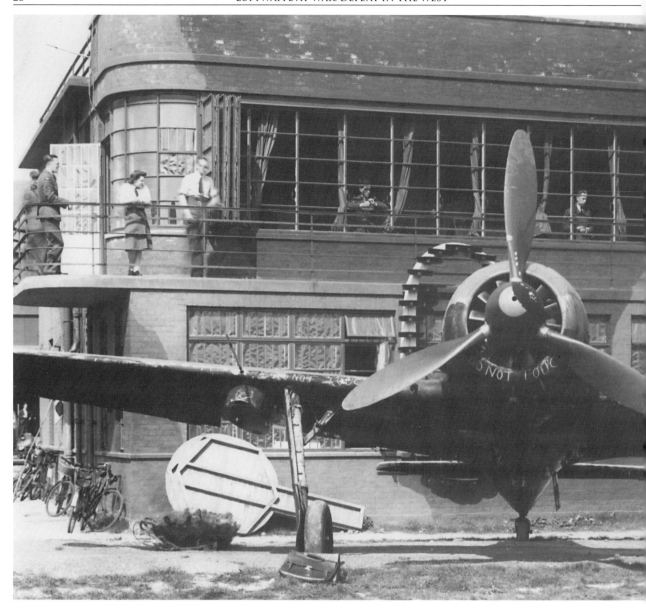

Left: Good condition, one rather careless owner. This FW 190A-4/U-8 of SKG 10 was one of those which landed inadvertently at West Malling on the night of 16/17 July 1943, after a raid on London. Night navigation was obviously not a strong point with SKG 10.

Opposite page, bottom: Among the best medium bombers of the war, the Junkers Ju 88 also saw service in reconnaissance and night fighter versions, and remained in service until the surrender. This shot-down example, one of several that night, fell in a recreation ground in London on the night of 17/18 March 1943.

Below: The most versatile *Luftwaffe* aircraft of World War II was arguably the Junkers Ju 88, which served in the bombing, anti-shipping, reconnaissance, ground attack and night fighter roles. Seen here is the Ju 88A-15, with an enlarged wooden bomb bay to increase internal carriage capacity.

Above: A direct development of the Junkers Ju 88E, the Ju 188 prototype was in fact the Ju 88 V-44, which differed from the original in having a remodelled nose, extended span pointed wings, and a larger, square-cut empennage. Powered by two BMW 801 radial engines, the first Ju 188Es entered service with 4/KG 66 and made their first operational debut over Britain on 18 August 1943.

Below: Designed to replace the He 111 and the Ju 88, the Dornier Do 317 was to have speed comparable with contemporary fighters and the range to attack anywhere in the British Isles. First flown in 1943, the Do 317 V 1 seen here differed from the Do 217M in having triangular fins. The project was abandoned late in 1943.

Opposite page, top: A close view of the extensively glazed nose of the Junkers Ju 188, which first flew in 1942. Like the Ju 88, this was also built in medium bomber, reconnaissance, torpedo bomber and night fighter variants. This is the Ju 188F-1 reconnaissance variant.

Opposite page, bottom: The Junkers Ju 188D-2 was a photographic reconnaissance variant equipped with FuG 200 search radar. These are aircraft of 1(F)/124, based at Kirkenes in northern Norway, which were tasked with finding targets for the torpedo bombers of KG 26.

Above: Larger aircraft were prodigal of resources, particularly light alloys. The Junkers Ju 352 *Herkules* represented an attempt to overcome this while meeting the demand for transport aircraft. Of mixed wood and steel construction with fabric covering, it reverted to the time-honoured trimotor configuration last used on the Ju 52m/3. One interesting innovation was an under-fuselage loading ramp which lifted the tail when lowered. A total of forty-three Ju 352s were built between October 1943 and September 1944.

Below: The Heinkel He 280 V1 first flew on 2 April 1941, the first jet aircraft ever to have been designed as a fighter. In direct competition with the Me 262, it was faster, climbed better, and had a higher ceiling. It failed to be adopted by the *Luftwaffe* primarily because its endurance was significantly less than that of the Messerschmitt jet, which itself was short enough.

Above: The Focke-Wulf FW 190A-5 appeared on the production lines early in 1943. A revised mounting allowed the engine to be carried about 15 cm further forward to alleviate overheating. Seen here is the A-5/U8 variant carrying a single SC 1000 bomb, one of the fins of which has been cropped to clear the ground. The A-5/U8 could operate as a long-range version when fitted with drop tanks.

Below: The final major production variant of the Focke-Wulf FW 190A series was the A-8, introduced at the end of 1943, which had increased fuel capacity. Its armament varied with sub-types. On the morning of D-Day, it was in FW 190A-8s that Josef Priller and his wingman flew the only *Luftwaffe* sorties over the invasion beaches.

Right: Although the Focke-Wulf FW 190 was a first-class air superiority fighter, it was also adaptable to other missions. This is the FW 190G fighter-bomber, which first entered service in February 1943. It is seen here carrying a 500 kg bomb beneath the fuselage and two 300 litre drop tanks beneath the wings.

Below: First flown at Oberpfaffenhofen in September 1943, the Dornier Do 335 *Pfeil* (Arrow), was the most radical of the conventionally-powered *Luftwaffe* fighters of the era, with two DB 601 engines located fore and aft; the former had an annular radiator which gave it the appearance of a radial engine. A reinforced ventral fin prevented the rear propeller from grounding on take-off. This is the Do 335 V-1 prototype.

Opposite page, bottom: The Junkers Ju 188A-3 appeared on the production lines in January 1944. Serving with II/KG 2, I/KG 6, and I/KG 66, the bomber variant Ju 188A-2 took part in Operation *Steinbock* in the first half of 1944. The example seen here is an A-3 of 2/KG 6, being loaded with torpedoes for anti-shipping operations.

Opposite page, top: A *Luftwaffe* fighter control station in the late war period, when accurate vectoring onto the American heavy bomber formations had become essential. The key was tracking and communications as shown here.

Opposite page, bottom: After sustaining damage from a British Anti-Aircraft Z (rocket) battery over Ealing, London on 23/24 February 1944, the crew of this Dornier Do 217M-1 of KG 2 baled out. The aircraft flew on, to make an almost perfect belly landing on allotments near Cambridge, almost 160 km away.

Above: Junkers Ju 188s damaged by USAAF bombing on Leipzig in February 1944. German aircraft production was severely hit by a series of heavy raids between February 1944 and April 1945.

Below: Excellent though the Focke-Wulf FW 190 was in the air superiority role, it was also in demand for attack, close air support, and even dive-bombing, and a great deal of production was devoted to these missions. The FW 190G was a dedicated fighter-bomber, which actually preceded the FW 190F into service. In essence, it was the FW 190A-5/U3, with strengthened main gear and reduced armament. The FW 190G-2 seen here differed from the G-1 in having Messerschmitt-designed bomb racks.

Left: In a fast-moving combat between fighters, instant identification was a constant problem, especially from head-on. Late in the war the *Jagdwaffe* adopted a spiral pattern on the spinner for easy recognition, as seen on this Messerschmitt Bf 109G. In the centre of the boss is the muzzle of the 30 mm cannon.

Top: An interesting weapon which failed to enter service was the Blohm und Voss BV 246 *Hagelkorn* (Hailstone) glider bomb, seen here beneath a Focke-Wulf FW 190G-8, probably of IV/KG 101. The bomb with its very high aspect ratio wing, seen here braced to the underside of the FW 190 wing, used radio direction finding to home on its target. Released at high altitude, its projected range was about 200 km.

Above: An interesting anti-bomber weapon tested on an FW 190A-8 was the SG 116 *Zellendusche*, consisting of six 30 mm vertical-firing MK 103 cannon, triggered by the shadow of a bomber falling upon a photo-electric cell. An attack was made by flying between 100 and 170 m below the bomber on an opposite heading. Like many other bright ideas, it didn't work very well.

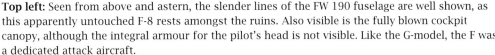

Top left: Seen from above and astern, the slender lines of the FW 190 fuselage are well shown, as this apparently untouched F-8 rests amongst the ruins. Also visible is the fully blown cockpit canopy, although the integral armour for the pilot's head is not visible. Like the G-model, the F was a dedicated attack aircraft.

Above: Defenders in the West: *Feldmarschall* Erwin Rommel, responsible for strengthening the Atlantic Wall against invasion, with *Oberst* Josef 'Pips' Priller (right), at that time *Kommodore* of JG 26, who gained more than 100 victories in the West.

Left: The Focke-Wulf FW 190F-9 (seen here with a flat tyre) was an anti-tank aircraft known as '*Panzerblitz*' or '*Panzerschreck*', which carried R4M rockets for its anti-armour role. Stub pylons for these can be seen under the wings. Few were built.

The most numerically important of the Messerschmitt Bf 109G series was the G-6. It was armed with a single 30 mm MK 108 cannon firing through the spinner, and two 13 mm heavy machine guns mounted above the engine. Bulges covering the machine gun breeches and ammunition feeds which gave the *Gustav* its nickname of *Beulen* (bumps); one is visible just ahead of the cockpit. It also boasted two 20 mm cannon in underwing pods. This example, formerly White 14 of JG 1, landed at Manston in the early hours of 21 July 1944.

Opposite page, top: A WGr 28/32 rocket projectile under the wing of a FW 190F. A large (28 cm diameter) shaped charge made this a very effective anti-tank weapon if it hit the target, but this this did not happen very often.

Above: As the Allies pressed forward across France in the second half of 1944, the *Luftwaffe* was forced to use temporary landing grounds. Here an FW 190A-8 is pushed back under cover among the trees.

Left: The final model of the Messerschmitt Bf 109G-series was the G-14, first revealed to the Allies when one was shot down by ground fire near Fontenay-le-Poesnel on 22 July 1944. Like many late model 109s, this has the clear-view 'Galland hood'.

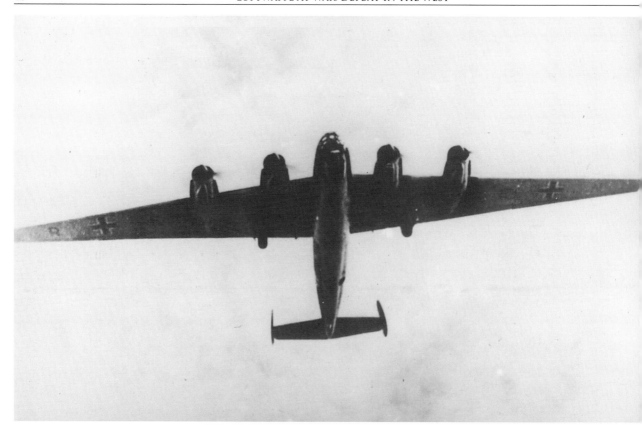

Opposite page, top: Designed to raid New York from Germany, the Messerschmitt Me 264V-1 prototype first flew in December 1942. However, the projected bomb load of 1800 kg was considered to be too small, and a six-engined variant was proposed. Meanwhile the Me 264V-1 was pressed into service as a transport, but was destroyed on the ground during an air raid late in 1944. No others were completed. It was the nearest the *Luftwaffe* got to producing a true strategic bomber. (*Mike Spick*)

Opposite page, bottom: The Heinkel He 177A *Greif* spear-headed the attacks on England in 1944 known as Operation *Steinbock*. The tactics were to approach the target area from the north, drop the bombs, then exit in a high-speed shallow dive. Seen here is an He 177A-5, probably of KG 100, captured by the French Resistance at Blagnac, near Toulouse, and brought to England in September 1944 for evaluation.

Above: The Heinkel He 177 *Greif* was a strange beast. It was powered by four engines, mounted side-by-side in pairs, each pair driving a single huge propeller. While this reduced drag and increased performance, cooling was inadequate, and overheating often resulted in engine fires. In addition, it had to be stressed for dive-bombing, which made the structure very heavy. Seen here is a He 177A-3 of KG 100 at Châteaudun early in 1944.

Below: Continual problems with the coupled engine installations on the Heinkel He 177 *Greif* led to the development of the He 274, powered by four individually installed DB 603A engines. First flown at Vienna-Schwechat late in 1943, the He 274V-1 (also known as the He 177B-0) suffered from directional instability. The demands of the emergency fighter programme caused the project to be cancelled on 3 July 1944.

Left: A sad-looking Heinkel He 177 shot down over England early in 1944. Like most *Luftwaffe* bombers, the crew was grouped in the nose for ease of co-operation, but the multi-paned nose transparencies were not very suitable for night operations, as they gave back confusing reflections from the instruments.

Opposite page, bottom: Briefly flown against the Allies following the Normandy landings, the Henschel Hs 129 was a dedicated attack aircraft. Heavily armed, and with a tiny armoured cockpit, the Hs 129 was underpowered, difficult to handle, and its presence on the Western Front passed almost unnoticed by the Allies.

Below: The need to accelerate pilot training from 1944, coupled with increasingly poor handling characteristics of the Messerschmitt Bf 109G, led to the adoption of a two-seater conversion trainer. This is the Bf 109G-12, converted from the G-5 airframe.

Above: In all, only 103 Junkers Ju 388s were built before production ceased early in 1945. Pictured is the Ju 388K-1 high altitude bomber, with a bulged wooden fairing beneath the fuselage to house the bomb load. Only five were completed.

Below: A heavy fighter which never quite made the grade was the Arado Ar 240A. First flown in 1940, it took part in operational trials over England during the following year, its high performance enabling it to escape interception. Plagued by instability, the programme was cancelled in 1942, but two aircraft remained in service into 1944, flying reconnaissance missions over England.

Opposite page, top: The forerunner of the modern cruise missile, the Fieseler Fi 103, also known as the V-1, the FZG 76, the *Kirschkern* (Cherrystone), and the Doodlebug, was used to start the last offensive against England, starting on 13 June 1944. Powered by an Argus pulse jet, reliability and accuracy left much to be desired, although the 848 kg high explosive warhead was very destructive.

Opposite page, bottom: When in the late summer of 1944 the Doodlebug launching sites in France had been over-run by the Allied armies, the only way of continuing the attack against England was to air-launch the weapons from beneath Heinkel He 111H-22s of III/KG 3, later redesignated II/KG 53. Navigational accuracy to the launch point was critical, and few V-1s thus launched found their target.

Beethoven was the codename for this pick-a-back arrangement, which consisted of a fighter controlling a war-weary bomber carrying a large explosive shaped charge. First used operationally on 25/26 June 1944, it was not a success, due to the near-impossibility of accurate aiming. This combination consists of Ju 88G controlled by a FW 190A-5.

Right: The Fieseler Fi 103R *Reichenberg* was a flying bomb, aimed at its target by a pilot who in theory was to bale out at the last second, but who in practice stood little chance of survival. Trials began in summer 1944, some piloted by the famous aviatrix Hanna Reitsch. While 175 were built, the *Reichenberg* was never used operationally, fortunately for both its pilots and the Allies.

Below: The Fieseler Fi 156 *Storch* was the most widely used *Luftwaffe* communications aircraft of the war. Its ability to fly slowly and to land in confined spaces was legendary. Used mainly in the West between 1943 and 1945 for picking up downed fighter pilots, a *Storch* made a memorable flight into Berlin during the final days of the war, piloted by Hanna Reitsch, carrying *Ritter* von Greim, the last *Luftwaffe* supreme commander, for a meeting with Hitler.

Opposite page, bottom: The Messerschmitt Bf 109K was the fastest variant of the type, capable of 720 km/h at 6000 m. Seen here at Munich in March 1945 is a Bf 109K-4, powered by the 1500 hp DB605ASCM engine; armed with two 15 mm and one 30 mm cannon, it had a pressurised cockpit for high-altitude interception.

The sleek lines of the Messerschmitt Bf
109K-6 conceal the fact that it was the most
heavily armed of all the 109 variants, with
three 30 mm MK 103 cannon and two 13
mm heavy machine guns.

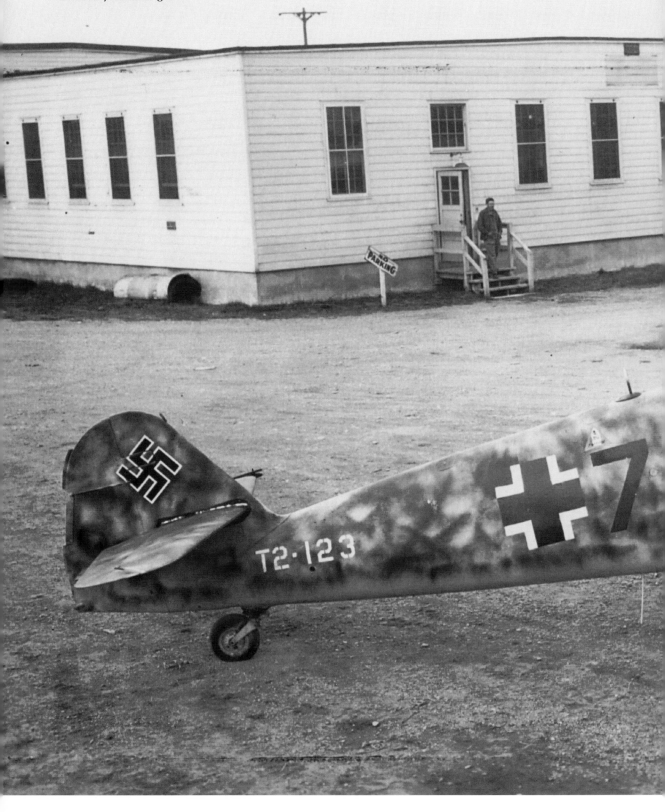

Above: Forward-swept wings was an idea before its time. They would postpone the drag rise at high subsonic speeds, while preventing tip stalling. The Junkers Ju 287V-1 seen here first flew on 16 August 1944, but wing flexing proved a problem which was not solved until the 1980s with the advent of aero-elastic tailoring using advanced composites.

Below: The FW 190D-9, the best conventional German fighter of the war. This late model features the fully-blown clear view cockpit hood. In the hands of an *Experte* it was deadly, but flown by a novice it was a turkey. Pilot quality rather than aircraft quality was the dominant factor in air combat.

Opposite page, top: The final Junkers bomber of the war was the Ju 388K-1, the V3 prototype of which is seen here.

The 3000 kg bomb load was carried in a bulged wooden housing beneath the fuselage. Only fifteen aircraft were buil before production ceased in 1945.

Opposite page, centre: The Messerschmitt Me 262A *Schwalbe* (Swallow) entered service in the autumn of 1944, making it the world's first operational jet fighter. Its overwhelming speed was an advantage in evading conventional fighters, but was embarrassing when attacking bombers as it gave too little firing time. (*Mike Spick*)

Opposite page, bottom: The original tailwheel arrangement of the Me 262 was less than satisfactory, and consequently this Messerschmitt Bf 109F-1, *Werke* Number 5603, was fitted with a fixed nosewheel as part of trials preceding the further development of the jet fighter.

Left: Repainted to represent EpGr 262, this Messerschmitt Me 262A-1a/U3 actually operated with *Sonderkommando Braunegg* from December 1944, flying the short-range reconnaissance mission, for which it was unarmed. Sheer speed made it virtually immune from interception.

Opposite page, bottom: Gun ports blanked out by the censor, this Messerschmitt Me 262A shows the slightly nose-high angle of attack needed on take-off. The *Schwalbe* had a slight sweepback on the wing leading edge, but not enough to be really significant in high-speed handling.

Below: The unreliability of German jet engines caused many accidents. While the Me 262 handled quite adequately at operational speeds with one engine out, asymmetric handling problems were extreme at low speeds, causing many accidents in the landing phase. The Me 262B-1a was a conversion trainer with an instructor pilot in the rear seat. Installation of the second seat reduced fuel tankage, and this model routinely carried drop tanks. (*Mike Spick*)

Above: The Arado Ar 234 *Blitz* was the world's first operational jet bomber. The *Blitz* first flew on 15 June 1943. Originally conceived to take off from a jettisonable trolley, and land back on a retractable skid, this arrangement proved impracticable and a wheeled undercarriage was added. A twin-engined single-seater, it entered service with KG 76 late in 1944.

Below: The Arado Ar 234 *Blitz* with its take-off trolley in position. While this arrangement worked moderately well from a smooth grass field, it was found to be generally impracticable. This is the Ar 234 V3, which was destroyed on an early test flight.

Opposite page, top: First flown on 8 April 1944, the Arado Ar 234 V6 was powered by four BMW 003A turbojets. It is seen here on its launching trolley, with the landing skid extended. It was the only four-engined single seat bomber ever designed. From September 1944 it was flown by *Sonderkommando Götz* in the reconnaissance role. (*Mike Spick*)

Opposite page, bottom: The Arado Ar 234 V8, powered by four BMW 003A turbojets in paired nacelles. First flown on 1 February 1944, it preceded the Ar 234 V6 by nearly seven weeks. Like the Ar 234 V6, it was flown by *Sonderkommando Götz* from September 1944. (*Mike Spick*)

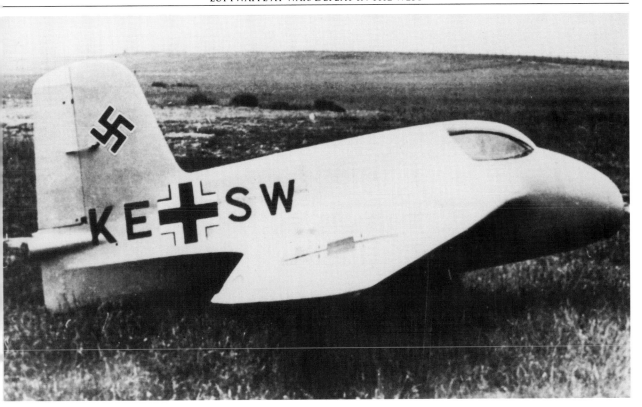

Opposite page, top: The Arado Ar 234C-3 was the only four-engined production variant. This featured a redesigned cabin with a raised roof to improve visibility, with two rearward-firing 20 mm cannon, and two forward-firing cannon beneath the nose. Five pre-production prototypes were built. (*Mike Spick*)

Above: The Messerschmitt Me 163V 1, a high-speed research aircraft seen at Peenemünde in the summer of 1941. Initial flight testing was carried out as a glider, before the rocket motor was fitted. At this time, there was little prospect of it being adopted as an operational fighter, but later events dictated otherwise.

Left: The Arado Ar 234B jet bomber was the first variant to have a conventional retractable undercarriage installed. The censor has blacked-out the unit markings on this aircraft. (*Mike Spick*)

Left: Often called the 'powered egg', the Messerschmitt Me 163B rocket fighter was developed as a fast-climbing point defence interceptor. Pleasant to handle, its two great weaknesses were short endurance and extremely volatile fuels. The former made it necessary to glide back to base, while the latter caused many accidents. (*Mike Spick*)

Opposite page, bottom: The Messerschmitt Me 163B *Komet* was the first tail-less fighter, and also the first rocket-propelled fighter, to enter production. This machine served with JG 400 at Brandis in the final months of the war. With engine-off, it could be dived at more than 800 km/h, making it far from a sitting duck even when out of fuel.

Below: One of ten Dornier Do 335A-0s built at Oberpfaffenhofen late in 1944. Of particular interest is the faceted windshield and canopy, which can have done nothing for the pilot's view. Before baling out, the rear propeller and tail fin were blown away by explosive bolts. At least one aircraft was fitted with a primitive ejector seat.

Opposite page, top: Dornier Do 335s under construction at Oberpfaffenhofen. Four raids by the USAAF between March 1944 and April 1945 reduced production significantly, and only eleven were delivered by the end of the war. Nearest the camera is a two-seater Do 335 conversion trainer.

Above: The Heinkel He 162 *Spatz* (Sparrow), unofficially known as the *Salamander*, was one of the first attempts at designing a lightweight austere fighter, mass-produced from non-strategic materials, and capable of being flown by novice pilots. Stressed for 7.5 g, with an ultimate load of 12.4 g, the *Salamander* was a 'hot ship', and in fact needed an experienced pilot to fly it. In combat it achieved virtually nothing.

Left: The ultimate Focke-Wulf FW 190 development was the Ta 152H, seen here on a compass-swinging platform at Cottbus in 1945. Similar in appearance to the FW 190D-9, for which it was often mistaken, the Ta 152H-1 had high aspect ratio wings and increased fuel capacity. It was capable of 755 km/h at 12,500 m. Only a handful entered service.

Above: In all, about 275 examples of the Heinkel He 162 *Volksjäger* were produced, of which a small proportion reached operational units. The war ended before these could become effective. This is an He 162A-2 of 2/JG 1.

Opposite page, top: The Blohm und Voss BV 155 started life as the Me 155 naval carrier fighter in 1942, was modified as a high speed bomber later that year, then was adopted as a high altitude fighter with a long span wing. Its first flight took place on 8 February 1945, but the project was overtaken by events.

Right: With the USAAF bomber formations tearing the Third Reich to pieces, desperation measures were in order. The design of the Bachem Ba 349 *Natter* (Viper) was begun in 1944 as a semi-expendable manned missile. Rocket-powered, it was launched vertically up a ramp. Armament was a battery of 73 mm unguided rockets; once these had been launched the pilot descended by parachute, as did the rear fuselage. The only known manned flight of the *Natter* ended in disaster, killing the pilot.

Above: Wing sweep was known to be critical at high speeds, and to investigate the best angle, Messerschmitt designed the P.1101, which could vary leading edge sweep between 35º and 40º on the ground. It never flew, but post-war it formed the basis of the Bell X-5 variable-sweep research aircraft.

Below: This Focke-Wulf FW 190D-9 was belly-landed at Rhein-Main airfield at the end of the war. Its shattered remains symbolise the end of an era for the *Luftwaffe*. This was the usual fate of surrendered aircraft, which were wrecked to prevent the Allies from capturing them intact. Fuselage markings indicate that it belonged to the *Stab* of an unidentified *Jagdgeschwader*.